intimates

grace crnojević

intimates

Is poetry like dirty laundry, or more similar to my intimates?

Provocative and true yet soft and delicate, words colored nude. Exposing most of myself but still within control, hope you can understand the sentiment. It's reflective of my being, it resembles myself, it's the language of my attitude. Dirty, clean, messy and elegant, no limits to how I write, I let my words complement my mood. In my safe space, where I feel the most affectionate. Thankful for my mind, I can't begin to explain my gratitude.

contents

black

disappear

How can they miss you
when you're always here?
This is when I must learn
how to disappear.

afterthought

Do you miss me?
I suppose not.
You can't really miss someone
who was always an afterthought.

fear

Now I have come to
the realization
you've just told me
what I wanted to hear.

Your intentions,
I don't understand them.
Your intentions,
they're not clear.

Now I'm face to face
with my biggest fear.
I am left alone,
with you no longer here.

dim

I am a cigarette
but you put me out.
I am every number
but you forgot how to count.

I am the whole ocean
but you're too scared to swim.
I am a star shinning bright
but you said you prefer it dim.

thorn

I always thought I was a rose,
soft and delicate.
Till you made me feel
like thorns in your side.

mathematics

I started to remove myself from the equation.
Just wanted to see if you'd even notice
a fraction of me was gone.

I know you noticed,
but never was there an attempt
to add me back.

And now your attention,
it is divided.
You've made me feel less than.

dirt

Sometimes I wonder,

"Do I not look like a person?"

Or do I look more like dirt
on the bottom of your shoes.

After you walked all over me.

running late

I've found the time to slow down,
and stand still in the middle of the street.

There I began to disassociate,
thinking maybe the sadness won't come back.

Turns out, it was just running late.

easy

I wish I could be easy.

It's not that complex of a theory to not take dying seriously because I began to think, if I must live in a world where compassion is obsolete and loneliness abundant, who would really bother anymore?

I used to run on a currency of empathy, love and authenticity and I kept giving it out, and after a while, I found myself bankrupt. But maybe it's not them, maybe it's just me. And maybe I'm just hard to love. I'm afraid I'll never been seen.

falling

It's terrifying to fall,
knowing there's no one to catch you.

I don't know what's more terrifying,
hitting the ground or if the falling never ends.

A continuous loop, a broken record,
on and on.

The more I discover myself, the more I'm afraid.

lost feelings

When the conversations became bland.
Lack of substance, nothing I can grasp in my hand.
I can't hold onto this, to me, you're made of sand.

abundance

I would think I would've gotten used to the hurt.
It's more familiar to me than anything else.
My feelings are too abundant,
my heart no longer on my sleeves
but it's my entire shirt.

cool

I lost my cool.
I guess I wasn't as cool
as you once thought.
And am I even a thought
in your mind?
And do you mind
if I don't talk for a while
because I won't feel better for a while.

I feel empty, I have no want. I want nothing.

personal

I took it personally,
because personally
I would never treat you
like you treated me.

Personally speaking...

retrograde

It's hurting me.
Retrograde again,
Mercury.

Life hasn't begun
but is already falling apart.
Do I give up, am I done?

Black and white, in the dark.
I'll keep trying,
but this time I've missed the mark.

How can I stop the spinning?
Going backwards,
my face thinning.

Feels like I'm running out of time,
didn't do anything, yet I feel guilty
like I've committed a crime.

I'm trying to not lose hope,
but it feels heavy, impossible
and I have unhealthy methods to cope.

Love is an art form that I haven't mastered yet.

loser

I'm a loser,
always a third wheel.
Laughing through the loneliness,
no one truly knows how I feel.
It seems like years,
and yet I'm still giving myself time to heal.
So much I've gone through,
often thinking this couldn't be real.
I'm growing up now, trying my best.
No one knows what's the deal,
yet they won't question me,
which makes it easier on me to conceal.
Friend or even lover,
whatever you're looking for, I'll be ideal.
Walls are already up,
it'll take a lot of work to break down this steel.
Keep knocking me down,
find me, break the seal.
Wondering why you're trying so hard,
wondering what's the appeal.

Sad teen turns into sadder adult. I don't know how to change. Maybe it's all my fault.

self-harm

I look at the scars on my arms,
wondering why I am so cruel to myself.
How can I betray my body,
the only thing that has always supported me.

I don't know what the appeal of self-harm was to me. If you asked me back then, the answers always changed.

Sometimes it was just an impulse with no second thought.

Sometimes it was trading one hurt for another.

But a lot of the time it was my way of showcasing the pain I felt on the inside, that was invisible to everyone else, into something visible. Like I was legitimizing my pain. Maybe everyone could finally see the pain I was going through was real. The pain was justified, or so I thought.

waking up

Can't believe there was a time,
when I couldn't wait to sleep
because it was another day closer to you.

Now I feel like not waking up,
not the next day,
not at all.

deadly

Not the pills.
Not the blades.
Not the drinks.

Loneliness is what kills.

How will I ever find the right person, if I haven't
found myself yet.

nothing

How are you able to make yourself feel something,
when you're hollow, low tank, empty?

All I'm feeling is nothing.

exhausted

I just want to stay home,
lie in bed and not move.
Mornings are difficult,
but the nights are worse.
Why is it so hard to exist.
I have no energy to live.

appetite

I have no appetite,
a diet of angel dust.
More than you,
there's something else I lust.

I want control, I want to choose.
It's not a need, it's a must.
I want to be so small I'd disappear.

Because when I see my image,
I can't help but be in disgust.
It's my brain, my eyes.
I don't know which one to trust.

grace crnojević

I feel like I'm too much and not enough all at once.

notice

I want you to notice when I am hurting,
but then again no I don't.
I hate having to explain myself,
but I do want you to know.
It's not fair to you, for me to expect you
to know what's going on in my head,
when I don't even have a clue.

Depression is:

Not changing your calendar from April to the current month of June.

Wanting to fall asleep in the bathtub.

Sleeping all day and feeling guilty about it.

Not feeling worthy to do the things you enjoy.

Holding your breath for long periods of time.

Not feeling the hot water bounce off your skin in the shower.

Inflicting yourself with small impulsive pains, pressing a safety pin to your skin or digging your nails into your thighs.

Not interacting with friends because you don't want to ruin their time.

Finding comfort in the hours of 1 – 6 am because the world doesn't feel real, in turn your problems don't feel real either.

Finding it difficult to put your empty coffee mug in the sink even though you're already walking to the kitchen.

sad poem

It's 3:39am and I'm sad.
Sad because when I'm in bed,
I turn to my right,
and only face the wall.

I am sad because
when we kiss,
it doesn't affect you,
the way it destroys me.

I am sad because
all we do is hold
conversations and
not each other.

Easy to get, easier to forget.

gone

I'll be going, but I'm not gone.
I'm still here.
Don't treat me
like I've already disappeared.

observant

I think I've concluded,
maybe I was only ever meant
to observe and not experience.

There's no amount of sleep that can remedy this kind of tired.

doubt

How can I not build doubt,
when your answers are short
as if there's nothing to talk about.

thin air

Don't force what's not there.
This love is invisible, thin air.

I don't feel it,
it's no one's fault
so why do I still feel like shit?

I was making tea once, and as the water was boiling, I had an intrusive thought. I had an impulse to touch the water, not necessarily to hurt myself but to see if I could feel something, anything! Because I felt nothing on the inside and I was so desperate to not feel numb anymore.

holding hands

I placed my hands together,
feeling the delicacy of my fingers,
the frail nature of my wrists.
Sometimes I feel like I want to break my hands,
so no one can ever hold
or let go of them again.

Nothingness makes you want to do the oddest of things. Like stick your hand in boiling water just to feel something. I don't know which hurts more, being burned or feeling nothing at all.

perspectives

I struggle to understand different perspectives.
To me, you were pale tinted piles of rose petals,
but to you, all you saw was a mess on the floor.
You were the ocean, the whole beach,
all you could say, was how much you hated sand.

irony

You were so scared to lose a girl like me,
so instead you let me go, *willingly*.

up

Maybe I wasn't enough but
the part that has me the most messed up,
is that you led my hand to open up,
then got tired of my talking, told me to shut up.
Leaving me with the damage of a heart that is
bruised and cut up.
All this truly feels fucked up.

I thought I was watering flowers, but I created downpours instead.

cold

There have been many nights, too many to count,
where I had to fall asleep with ice on my chest
because my heart was physically hurting.
It was the only way to soothe the pain.
Yet you have the nerve to ask me,
why I've turned so cold.

imposter syndrome

I struggle with making an honest connection.
My aura, my subconscious, I'm limited.
Not out of a fear of rejection,
I think it's my need to control,
it's a consequence of wanting protection.

What I really want, what I really desire
is having someone who yearns for my affection.
What I want and what I look like on the outside,
when I look in the mirror,
I don't recognize the reflection.
I don't know her,
how I envision myself
isn't what I see.

crying

Don't know when,
I decided to keep my tears in.
I'm scared to let it begin,
Because once I start,
I don't know when
the crying will end.

I can feel the dark circles under my eyes. They hurt; it hurts.

Cigarette smoke triggers my memories like
nothing else. Reminds me of being a child, you'd
smoke, and smoke and I loved you so much, I'd
cry please, begging you to quit. I was so scared to
lose you. You'd laugh it off, and say, "I'm not
going anywhere.". From childhood to early teens, I
traded in each birthday wish, hoping and praying
you'd quit. Didn't you love me enough to quit?

Finally, after ten years or so I quit having hope, I
knew you loved me, but I accepted it. I stopped
hiding lighters, because you'd just buy new ones.
Maybe you'd be right all along like you were
about everything else, that magically cancer would
never find you. You were always healthy; never
had a scare, nothing was ever wrong.

So, when you died, it was hard to cry. I knew it. I
knew it would happen and for the first time in my
life I wish I wasn't right. Maybe that's why I cried
so hard as a child, I was already mourning you as
if I was already cementing this premonition as
truth. So now that you did go somewhere, all I can
feel is anger. You lied. You never tried, and you're
gone but we are here in pain. Just like when I was
a child, smoking was a pleasure to you, but I was
crying myself to sleep, my 8-year-old body full of
anxiety before I even knew what anxiety was
because I knew you'd die before you even
attempted to quit for good.

You'll never have the opportunity to walk me
down the aisle, you'll never meet the grandkids
you deserved to have, you'll never have the

chance, didn't you think of these things every time you lit a cigarette?

So now when I smell cigarette smoke, I am sad because a part of me wishes it was from you. You died because you smoked, and I'd die just to see you smoke again.

lamb

I can't help but still hold you when you cry.
In that moment it's not about me,
I just want you to be okay, I can't help but try.

I should be mad at you
but I will never stop caring.
I just wish you'd care about me too.

It's in my nature, it's just who I am.
Sometimes I wish I can cut the wires,
change my mind's program.

Back to a naive girl,
innocent as a lamb.

debt

Lack of energy, none left.
No more funds, I'm in sleep debt.
The more I sleep, the worse it is.
What can I do, haven't figured it out yet.

Head down on this table,
all I can see is my hair, brunette.
Covering my face, finally I doze,
then wake up in a cold sweat.

I would like to turn back,
roll me back like a cassette.
Just kiss my forehead,
and leave it wet.

speak

I have a lot to say,
but no opportunity to speak.
My words slowly inching out,
like a faucet leak.
My outward appearance shy,
vacant, unapproachable and meek.
Waiting for someone to listen,
holding this burden and I am weak.
I may not be ordinary,
but don't treat me like a freak.
Take a look inside me,
go on and take a peek.
You see me for who I am,
no longer shrouded in this mystique.

I'm not inspired,
I'm just fucking tired.

word

Not sure
which hurts more.
No longer talking,
or you don't care
if we never shared
another word.

I don't think people who don't experience clinical depression can comprehend that yes, I am aware I am sad and depressed and theoretically I could just "think about something else" but depression is an obsession. I often compare it to being possessed. I am 100% aware that I am acting a certain way and I just cannot stop. I can't look away from the car crash.

I get sadder and sadder and I'm so aware of that fact but it's an out of body experience. You break your hand, you know it's broken, and it hurts but no matter the willpower and awareness you may have, being aware doesn't magically fix your hand. Physical and mental pain are both real, except people are more sympathetic towards one more than the other. I'm sure you can guess which one.

Then the guilt pours salt on the wound. I'm already down and now I'm kicked in the stomach of feeling guilty for how I'm behaving as if I had a choice. Who the fuck would choose to be depressed? But even being aware of this and even being able to put exactly how I feel into words, you can bet that I will still feel this guilt.

I'm not asking for your advice, not looking for a quick fix, I just want you to understand as best as you can, an open ear says a lot more than any words of advice.

gray

My life feels like the spectrum of black to white with the gray areas in between. Although life can feel like it's either black or white in terms of certainty, but no one talks about the middle enough, how it feels and what does gray area mean. If it's not happy, is it sad? But that's not how gray is. Gray could be the healing, it could be the realization, it can be the slippery slope into despair or a breakthrough towards the light. If anything, gray feels like every day.

candle

My feelings are not a switch,
there is no on and off.
My feelings are more like a candle,
I burn for a long time,
but when I'm out,
I'm out…

indefinitely.

too much

I think too much
but don't think too much of myself.
I should put that energy towards me
and not someone else.

Is it easier when I'm not there, pretending to not care? Tell me are you afraid to feel?

flow

There is something in my nature
that makes me want to stand up
and go against the current
but then act surprised when I find myself
thrusted back, head held under;
lungs full of water till I'm left drowning.

Going with the flow…

grasp

Your hand has weakened,
what was once made from iron
now feels like glass.

Finally, I was able to escape
between your fingers,
no longer in your grasp.

kerosene

My deepest feelings are going unseen
burning me from the inside out,
feels like I'm covered in kerosene.

But there you are.
I'm addicted, like you were caffeine.
Maybe I can continue living here,

existing in the in between.

purgatory

I've always felt like my life was a purgatory.
Stuck between reality
and the places I wanted to be.

On the outskirts of happiness,
drowning in the middle of the sea,
voiceless, forgotten, no one beside me.

ambiguity

This part of my life is called,
"Doing what I know best."
Keeping how I feel on the down low,
my feelings are now ambiguous.

Truthfully, I've became good at healing myself.
After all I've had to do it time after time.
But how many times can a broken soul mend?
I hope I don't have to find out again.

heart

My heart had gone through a metamorphosis,
it was kind, it was new.
Ready to open and let in love,
but such is life.

Anxiety filled the voids,
with self-doubt and assurance that I was too naïve,
to think anyone could be authentic with me.
At a last attempt to survive, my heart had to
protect itself.

I could feel the brick and plaster harden,
the walls going up, the knot in my throat solid.
My heart was growing hard, and it seemed there
was nothing I could do to prevent this.

This helplessness is what keeps me up at night,
will it forever be like this? Will I turn cold?
And how can I come back from this?
How many times is enough?

Pure like a diamond,
cut and rough,
hard to the touch yet still precious.
This is now my heart.

afraid

Are you afraid of something real?
Is it easier to move on
than to let yourself heal?

stronger

I dislike the theory, one must be given obstacles in
life to condition themselves, to become stronger.

"What doesn't kill you makes you stronger!"
they'll say.

But what would they say next when I respond,
"Sometimes I don't want to be strong."

And then it makes me really wonder,
"Well, what if it does kill you?"

No one really deserves that, to feel that burden.
Is life just nothing but one big Pavlov lesson?

I say, "To hell with that."

thick skin

I prayed every night for strength, my skin thicker.
Fantasizing about the day I'll stop caring,
having the satisfaction of living free.

That day has come but I'm mourning my softness,
not because it's gone but because now it is tainted.

It's hard when you're responsible for your only source of happiness and you're not strong or willing enough to take on that role.

neon

Finding love in neon lights,
drinking like you're on endless funds,
trying to avoid those sleepless nights.

Because when you're feeling so low,
even a step can bring you to new heights.
Exit signs found everywhere you turn,
on inhale, you'll soon be high as kites.

You're only mad at the ones you love,
feels like lifetimes of ongoing fights.
I'm young and misunderstood.
I'm not bad, I'm just trying to feel alright.

tick

When you're sad, the days feel so long.
Each minute ticks for hours,
can't help feeling like something is wrong.

When you're happy, the days are a blink.
Can't even comprehend the details,
have no time to think.

selfish

Am I really acting selfishly?
Because every once and a while,
I only want to act accordingly
and do things
that only benefit me?
I feel so guilty to admit this,
but why do I have to behave secretly?
It kills me that most of my life is for others,
My soul aches because it's not free.

coffee

I drink too much coffee,
and sing bad.
I want to wear nothing,
because I am sad.

I need a little touching,
waiting for you to drive me mad.
Please, again remind me,
why you're the best I've ever had.

full

Holding my head, it feels full.
All these thoughts I have,
I am so emotional.

Push and pull,
thanks for understanding,
I know I can be a handful.

I'm dreaming of being the girl of your dreams.

girl

You finally found out,
what I've known from the start.

You may like other girls,
but you'll never find another girl like me.

hurt

You have to let it hurt,
hurt deeply and hurt loudly.
You have to feel it,
and remember it.
So that when you're finally healed,
and you will heal,
that you will be liberated.
You'll realize you can do anything,
and it's no longer scary to do so.
If you survived that,
you will do everything.

alone

I'd rather be lonely,
than settle for someone who
makes me feel alone.

concept

I'm a passerby in a crowd; a Paris lady.
Making unintentional eye contact,
daydreaming if I'll ever be someone's baby.

Keep thinking of me as only a concept,
nothing more in depth,
in return to you,
I'm only a secret best kept.

as two

I feel like I can't enjoy my favorite things alone.
I want to know what it feels like,
walking this city as two.
Turn all my old memories into new,
will that happen for me?
If not with you, then who?
I want it so bad, I'm at a loss for words.
I don't know what else I can do.

playing cards

Sometimes you have to admit,
The cards life had dealt you
are nothing but shit.

Do you keep playing?
You lose and lose.
Isn't it easier to just quit?

coping mechanisms

My only way of coping,
is to write poems and hoping
you'll read them one day.

I spend more time daydreaming than living.

wrong

Even if the timing was wrong,
I still wish I gave it my all.
I knew so many before and after you,
yet memories of them I can't recall.

99¢ dreams

Disassociating city walking,
a shop window, poster up,
on sale again, 99 cent dreams.
Phone full of missed calls,
I need space,
a galaxy wouldn't be enough.
Another coffee ordered in midtown,
the rain droplets are racing,
and I'm ready for another.
Why is today different than yesterday,
why can't I focus?
I keep walking aimlessly but feel no relief,
from this feeling of being in the clouds.
Ground me, grind me, like these coffee beans.
Maybe tomorrow, I'll wake up back in reality.

nice

My first instinct is to be nice,
but thanks to you,
I now think twice.

sweet nothings

It's hard to believe what people say,
like how you said you loved me
but were gone the next day.
Sweet nothings really mean nothing,
I'm just bored now so I'll listen anyway.

not your girl

You want me in your world?
I refuse to bend and curl.
Fuck being your girl.

It's amazing what magic a hot bath is. Lying in the bath, I lay to my side and touch the cold tile walls. I love the contrast of hot water and cold tile, I can feel it, it feels real. This makes me reflect on what a burden being an empath is. I hurt all the time, if I'm not hurting for my own sake, it is for someone else's. We're never meant to stay cold yet why do I always feel subjected to that? Is life forever cruel?

Now, life doesn't feel as cruel, but I also don't feel any warmer than this now room temperature bathwater. Lukewarm is how I'm feeling lately.

okay

I'll be okay
because I'm always just okay.
But for once I'd like to be
more than okay.

I want to be happy and finally join
the elite group of happy goers
I want to know that life.

I want to smile,
not because I'm disguising a frown.
I'd like to smile just because.
Because life is just that great.

What is it like to be happy to be alive?

I must stay self-contained if I want to keep myself sane.

forward

I will move forward,
I can't keep myself in this place.
I'm moving slowly,
better pick up my pace.
I have to make it out alive,
even with tears running down my face.

make my day

You simultaneously make
or ruin my day.
If your intentions aren't good,
then please stay away.

full cup

I forgot why I loved getting fucked up,
my state of mind flips
and now my empty glass is a full cup.

I'm no longer thinking of you on my lips.
Finally feeling comfortable
with someone else's hands on my hips.

mean

I just want you to be mean.
Make me believe you really don't care.
So, I can start to hate you,
I feel like that's the only way it's fair.

run away

I've always had an impulse to run away,
just keep running.

I've always wondered what it was like,
to meet someone who made me want to stand still.

Can I find happiness in my loneliness? Will I ever find comfort?

walk away

Choked up,
at a loss of what to say.

Even given the opportunity,
I would still walk away,

I won't go back to the way it was,
pretending I was okay.

climax

I covered my face
during the moment.
Couldn't let you see
when I was the most vulnerable.

lost

Waiting at this station,
where am I going?
What is my destination?

A bullet train to the future,
please give me that instant gratification.
I'll obsess unless it's now.

Anxiety starts, can't shake this fixation.
Point A to B, it begins and never ends.
Forever on rotation.

What would I say to my new self?
I think we're lost in translation.

I remember once you told me you liked the color
on my lips. I wore that lipstick for months.

revolving

I wish you saw me as a real woman,
and not as a revolving door.
Please if you want to go,
keep it that way.

But if you ever choose to come back,
then all I ask, the only request,
that this time you'll stay.

shallow

All my life I have felt
like the deep end of a pool.
Everyone is tempted to dive in
till the realize they cannot swim.

Sorry if I'm not shallow enough for you.

i don't care

When I needed you most you were not there.
Now that you're back, crying to me,
remind me why it's my responsibility to care.

I've turned to ice, definition of cold.
You can keep apologizing,
continue easing your guilt.
Doesn't mean I'll give in; this time I will not fold.

"Why are you so cold?"

It is the result of being taken advantage of. My mind and heart are trying desperately to save themselves. It's hard to be kind when it's been a long time since someone has been kind to you.

I wasn't trying to purposefully be this way, I was just trying to give myself space to heal yet ironically, I was still hurting or unintentionally hurting someone else in the process. Forgive me, I'm trying to change. I don't want to be this way.

Maybe it's not that I've forgotten how to be lovely. I just felt like I didn't deserve to be perceived that way. I felt awful so I was being awful. I promise I will teach myself to be warm again.

skeleton

Sometimes sugar makes it easier
to swallow medicine.

Sometimes I let you hurt me,
because I thrived off the adrenaline.

Honestly, I don't know what I'd say
if we ever met again.

All I know is this time I'd be different,
finally, you'd see me as genuine.

Wonder if you'd find me more alluring,
my energy more feminine.

You'd pay for my drink,
like a perfect gentleman.

Would you find your way back
inside of me, replacing my skeleton?

happiness

Happiness is possible,
I've felt it before.
Pained at the thought
and not quite sure
if I have it in me,
to try anymore.

I do want it, deep in my core.
Like a sea salt wave,
Crashing on the shore,
withdrawing shortly after,
sinking to the ocean floor.

Happiness like the jewelry I wore.
Doesn't have to be so complex,
no more abstract than bedroom décor.
The thought of giving it another go,
it's a feeling I have, no longer can ignore.

art

I'm not her,
I won't break your heart.
Why end this,
before it can even start?
We could make masterpieces,
you and I are pieces of art.
You don't have to change for me,
because I love every part.

bizarre

Radio humming on low,
kissing in your car.
Doesn't matter to me,
I just want to be where you are.

I'm the moon,
and you're my star.
You loved that I'm crazy,
unique and a little bizarre.

In hindsight you played my heartstrings
like your personal guitar.
Now leaving me wondering if you think of me,
wondering if I'm even on your radar.

lukewarm love

Give me none or give me your all,
I have no use for some.
Close your eyes and just fall
in love with me and come
to the realization you need no one else.

patient

Please be patient,
I'm not new to this feeling,
it's not quite foreign more like adjacent.
I'm just insecure,
but not unwilling, I'm fully complacent.
Move slow with me,
please be patient.

whatever

I don't care.
That's a lie
But not quite.
If whatever was a mood,
then that's what I'm feeling.
Whatever to the past,
whatever to the roads ahead
and whatever to the wherevers
it might take me.

"Whatever" feels like the anthem of survival.

done

Are you aware of what you do to me?
Can't think of anyone else.
You're more than the one,
I don't want to look anymore,
please I want to be done.

I miss you.
But I'd still
cross the street
to avoid you.

garden

If you want a garden,
you also have to accept
when it rains.

circles

Dark hair, dark circles,
I'm tired of our conversation,
I'm tired of talking in circles.

I *left* because you weren't *right* for me.

fight

Manifest, pray, cast a spell.
Do what you must,
I'm preparing to fight like hell.
I'm going all out,
I'm escaping this depression cell.

Sometimes I have to remind myself that this
current situation, this current life, isn't forever.
Every day I am allured and reassured by the idea
of disappearing. On my commute home from
work, I pass by the airport, I tempt myself with the
idea of finally escaping, I'm facing that runway
and have a "never looking back" type of feeling.
I don't know why I think running away would
solve anything, I'm confident it wouldn't solve
everything if anything. My thoughts spin like
spider threads, creating webs, and like the purpose
of webs, I am stuck, stuck in this way of thinking.
Just a chapter, just a chapter in the book of my life.
It will not last forever. There has to be a time when
one chapter finishes so the next one can begin.
This is not it, it's not the end.

white

Do you ever touch the skin on your face and drag your fingertips across your cheek just to reassure yourself that you're real? I'm not as sad as I was but the depression and anxiety are still present just dormant, lingering waiting to rear their ugly heads. Feels like the calm before a storm. Life finally feels worth living yet I'll have an impulse to crash my car, these feelings will never go away forever. This is who I am, but it is okay. It's okay because I'm not going to allow it to be all that I am. I'm a writer, an artist, someone who deserves a happy life.

I'm not ashamed of my mental illnesses, I just am thankful I've found my outlet. I just need to write more, not just about the bad but also the good too.

strawberries and cream

Every word I want to scream
with truths sugar coated
like strawberries and cream,
meant only for you to eat.
Soft and delicate between your teeth,
you told me they tasted sweet.

spine

My shoulder, still wet from your kiss,
and when your finger traces down,
the tension is felt upon my spine
as if I was now yours
and you just signed the dotted line.

dancing

I love to dance,
sway my hips.
Hair between my fingertips.

I feel beautiful,
out there on the dance floor,
making them all wonder,

"Who is she dancing for?"

sure

Reassure, reassure.
You asked me, "am I sure?"
I replied, "what for?"

"Are you ready for more?
because I want to make you sore."
I exhaled deeply, "I'm sure."

deep

When you speak, it's so deep,
both your words and voice.
Smooth and silky, lulls me to sleep.
I can't hold them down,
my feelings are starting to creep.
I know this is real,
because of the way you make me weep.

thinking of you

My rose blossoms,
the petals, please touch them.
Don't mind the thorns,
my petals are wet with dew,
my petals are wet thinking of you.

I'm scared of change,
but what scares me more than change,
is staying exactly where I am.

I am terrified of not changing at all.

wings

My arm stretches, reaching back,
trying to find my invisible wings.
Instead, I touch scratches you left behind,
I love them even though they still sting.
You love my body more than I ever have,
and I love when you pull my hair like string.
You are it, the one,
you are everything.

tightly

Hold me tightly,
I feel your fingertips.

Sing to me softly,
and I'll kiss your lips.

I want to see you nightly,
my moon with no eclipse.

Don't take me lightly,
keep your hands on my hips.

I'm not exactly where I want to be,
but I am further than I was.

creative outlet

My only reflex is to create.
Create when I hate,
create to change the state
of mind I'm in.
Create memories and dates,
create till happiness comes back,
even when it's running late.
My fate, my fate, it's what I am.
If nothing else, I will create.

pain

There's a slight pain,
every time my forehead
is hit by your gold chain,
when you're on top.
But who am I to complain?
You're so attractive,
sweat mixed with champagne.
Do that thing I like,
drive me wild, make me insane.

morning

Rise and shine,
waking up next to you
and this empty bottle of wine.
Clothes scattered on the floor,
can't remember if this shirt is yours
or mine.

worth it

11th floor room, looking out the window.
I'm on top,
and you're below.

Counting the city lights, one, two.
When you look at me, what do you see,
what am I to you?

My face rests in your hand,
I'm weak in my knees,
catch me, I can no longer stand.

I don't care if this moment came late,
It's us now,
you made it worth the wait.

wife

I want you for life,
be your last kiss.
I want to be your wife.
I'm not even good at cooking,
but for you, I'd pick up a knife.

you care

I notice all the details,
like the way your hand looks,
when you grip the steering wheel.
You like driving fast,
but you told me not to worry.
You'd go slow for me,
because you know it scares me.
The little things you do that show
how much you care for me.

Playing all my favorite records and for the record,
you're my favorite.

spite

Despite it all,
I can't help but smile.
Maybe it's to spite it all.
I'm more fucking powerful
than you'll ever know.

I've always felt like whatever I did, I had to have a purpose behind my motives. I felt like I could not do something with just half my heart. To me, the most precious thing is my energy and how I spent it because of my natural lack of it. My energy is precious, if I give you mine, please understand that you in turn are even more precious to me.

When I write, it's because I have something to let out.

When I kiss, it's because there is a passion I have inside of me.

When I walk, it's because I need to keep moving forward.

When I love, it's because I want to finally let my walls down.

I do wish that I didn't always feel this need to have a purpose. But by having purpose at least when I die, I can feel like I never didn't do what I wanted to do in that moment. Well, I hope at the very least.

beautiful again

With the scars on the small of my back,
I was always insecure if anyone would ever
find me beautiful again.

With healed fractured bones,
that would never be the same.
I wondered if I could perform for you
without being in immense pain.

Thank you for touching me,
making me forget those things,
you've made me feel beautiful again.

bitter

You used to call me semi sweet,
because you always thought I was bitter.
It's not that I was being unreasonable,
I just wanted better.

stressed

Maybe we would be less stressed
if we undressed.

Clothes spilled on the floor,
it's not enough, I want more.

tease

It's true, you make me weak in the knees.
You came close to my soul,
but didn't quite have the keys.
It's not entirely your fault,
even to my own self I'm quite the tease.
In your mind, I occupy too much space,
don't even have to pay rent or any other fees.
There is no other truth to this reasoning,
it's just that I like you, but I love me.

starstruck

After I caught a glimpse of you,
a little star got caught in my eye.
It did not burn or hurt,
but still I began to cry.
Puddles of galaxies pooled
on my cheek with visions
of you and I,
embracing and swirling
up above the world so high.

strangers

What a pleasure it has been
to let enough time pass
so that now you're a stranger again.

Promising we'd remain friends,
both lying through our teeth.
Now we no longer have to pretend.

Thankful it has all came to an end,
proud you no longer have the right,
to ever refer to me as your girlfriend.

sweet and sour

Sweet and sour,
when I'm with you,
I don't want to even waste an hour.
Everything I do, it's because I want to.

I don't want to stop,
not till my apartment becomes ours.
You pick me up, I'm on top.
Together we'll hide away, to our ivory tower.

fate

You look at my face, my eyes are wide.
You see me for who I am,
I don't even know what to say, I am tongue tied.

I'd be lying if I said I didn't want to be by your
side.
I want to touch you,
let you between my thighs.

Red strings of fate, our pinkies tied.
Even with our nights full of sin,
my body is left purified.

manhattan

In my ear you kiss me in Latin,
my hair caught between your fingers.
You play rough yet have a voice soft a satin.
Even when you're not here, your essence lingers.
Come back home, upper east side Manhattan.

unclasp

Your voice in the morning,
all raspy.
This captures my attention,
grasps me.
I begin to get up,
you grab me.
Come back please,
you unclasp me.

closer

Shoulder to shoulder,
wondering what I can do
to get our skins even closer.

So close I feel the friction,
sorry if I ask again,
you're just my addiction.

It's happy tears I cry,
when I look at you,
I'm so happy I could die.

expressions

What expression does my face have,
when I'm mad,
when I cry,
when it's inches from yours?

I want to live inside your head,
I want to know your thoughts,
and how do see me,
and where do you want to touch me?

What goes through your mind,
I'm dying to know.

beach

I have a feeling you find me cute,
as my face turns from pale to peach.
Salt air filing our lungs,
spending our day at the beach.
Sunkissed with freckles,
glitter dusted on my shoulders,
on my skin; speckled.

able

Everything I want to do,
feels tangible.

I don't know how to explain it,
but I feel capable.

Every doubt I was feeling,
has become short of laughable.

Don't stop me now,
I'm on fire, I'm flammable.

linger

I'm catching myself holding my breath,
I don't want it to be over,
I'm no longer praying for death.
But I'd still follow you to hell,
I'm an angel but where you go,
I too will dwell.
Strings wrapped around our fingers,
sometimes they might get tangled,
but our energies forever linger.

the best

Freckles on my nose,
my skin's soft,
like petals on a rose.

Strawberry cake,
my pouted lips,
for you to take.

Hands tugging on my hair,
pull gently,
treat me with care.

Kiss me where it hurts,
and where it doesn't.
Reach underneath my shirt.

Love to hear my cry,
in this moment,
I feel like without you I'd rather die.

I feel like I can't get close enough,
you know your baby,
and how she likes it rough.

Head laying on your chest,
I hear your heart echoing,
reminds me why I love you the best.

love language

"This made me think of y.."
I can't even let you finish your sentence,
because I'm in love with you.
I don't even care what it was
that made you think of me,
I just can't believe you think of me,
even when you're not physically with me.

therapy

I only need one type of therapy,
it's the one where you call me baby,
you kiss my forehead and never leave me.

for me

I write expecting no one to read,
I draw expecting no one to see,
I create because it's a need,
I sing so I can feel free.

sunset

Our bodies tinted by the sunset,
you never looked so beautiful.
Your face I'll never forget.

chance

If you'd give me the chance,
I promise you I'd love you
like no one ever has
like no one else can.

If you'd give me this dance,
I'll make you feel
like no one ever has,
like no one else can.

dizzy

I'll take you on a dizzy honeymoon,
keep you awake all night,
snoozing the alarm till noon.
I act like I don't care,
but my love is in full bloom.
Want a taste of my angel dust?
Eat me by the spoon.

charm

Wondering how you got a stubborn girl like me
to fall into your arms.
It's like how you get everything else,
you use those boyish charms.
And everything I know about men like you
was swiftly thrown aside leaving me disarmed.
But I knowingly gave in,
I thought what possibly could be the harm?

fun

Walk, don't run.
Warmth on my cheeks,
thank you, Sun.
It's not over,
I'm not done.
I'm just going slow,
I'm just having fun.

poems & cover art by:
grace crnojević

find more at:
author:
@grace.crnojevic

instagram &tiktok:
@gracecrnojevic.poetry

website:
gracecrnojevicpoetry.com

bio

Grace Crnojević is a New Orleans born, Sarasota raised poet/writer. Grace has been writing since a young age, even having her first poem published in her school's newspaper at the age of 7 and at age 10 starting a poetry club. By incorporating multiple mediums of written word, photography, cinematography and artwork all done by Grace, she hopes to bring something new to the world of poetry. Raw, comedic, honest and empathy are all tones found in Grace's work.

www.gracecrnojevicpoetry.com

ISBN: 979-8-218-24674-7

Library of Congress Control Number: 2023912936

Cover Design by Grace Crnojević